TEACH Teenagers to PRAY

A 4-week course to help senior highers explore the depth and excitement of real prayer

by Michael Warden

Loveland, Colorado

Group®

Teaching Teenagers to Pray
Copyright © 1994 Group Publishing, Inc.

Credits
Edited by Stephen Parolini
Cover designed by Liz Howe and Amy Bryant
Title designed by Diana Walters

11 10 9 8 7 6 5 4 3   04 03 02 01 00 99 98 97
ISBN 1-55945-407-5
Printed in the United States of America.

CONTENTS

Teaching Teenagers to Pray

Lesson 1	9

What Is Prayer?

Students will learn how to pray more effectively and create their own prayer journal.

Lesson 2	18

Private Prayer

Students will learn how to pray alone and plan a private prayer time with God.

Lesson 3	25

Team Prayer

Students will learn how to pray together and go in teams to pray for others.

Lesson 4	31

Corporate Prayer

Students will learn about corporate prayer and design a concert of prayer for the congregation.

Bonus Ideas	38

Introduction
TEACHING TEENAGERS TO PRAY

In an age of transcendental meditation, spirit guides, and drug-induced spiritual journeys, prayer has become an enigma to many young people. Besides the competing "roads" to greater spirituality, kids deal with a strong undercurrent of fear when it comes to prayer—especially when praying out loud.

After all, it can be a terrifying thing to come before the presence of an all-powerful God. What should you say? How should you speak? How can you possibly consider yourself good enough to even approach God?

This action-based course on prayer tackles all of these struggles head-on by helping kids see that God is both powerful and merciful, just and forgiving, vast and personal. These four meetings lead kids through several personal and group encounters with God, teaching them not only the basics of prayer, but also focusing on the ultimate goal of prayer—unity with Christ.

Some of your students will be excited to dive into the experiences prescribed in this course. Others will be a bit more apprehensive. That's OK. Encourage those students who are uncomfortable that we're all in a process of growth, and none of us has yet arrived spiritually. Remind all your students that God is willing to give them the freedom to try new things, to grow at their own pace, and to do it all without fear of judgment from others—or from themselves.

Use this course to help your teenagers discover how to pray effectively in all of life's circumstances and discover the power and peace prayer can bring to their lives.

COURSE OBJECTIVES

By the end of this course, your students will
- discover exactly what prayer is,
- keep a personal prayer journal of their experiences with God,
- go on a private excursion with God,
- pray with a team of people for a special group or person, and
- design and lead a prayer concert for the congregation.

THIS COURSE AT A GLANCE

Before you dive into the lessons, familiarize yourself with each lesson aim. Then read the Scripture passages.

- Study them as a background to the lessons.
- Use them as a basis for your personal devotions.
- Think about how they relate to kids' circumstances today.

Lesson 1: WHAT IS PRAYER?

Lesson Aim: Students will learn how to pray more effectively and create their own prayer journal.

Bible Basis: Philippians 4:6-7 and James 5:13-18.

Lesson 2: PRIVATE PRAYER

Lesson Aim: Students will learn how to pray alone and plan a private prayer time with God.

Bible Basis: Matthew 14:23; Mark 1:35; Luke 5:16; and 6:12-13.

Lesson 3: TEAM PRAYER

Lesson Aim: Students will learn how to pray together and go in teams to pray for others.

Bible Basis: Luke 9:18, 28 and Ephesians 6:18.

Lesson 4: CORPORATE PRAYER

Lesson Aim: Students will learn about corporate prayer and design a concert of prayer for the congregation.

Bible Basis: John 17:20-23 and Acts 2:42-47.

HOW TO USE THIS COURSE

PROJECTS WITH A PURPOSE™ for Youth Ministry

Think back on an important lesson you've learned in life. Did you learn it by reading about it? from hearing a lecture about it?

Chances are, the most important lessons you've learned came from something you experienced. That's what active learning is—learning by doing. And active learning is a key element in Group's Projects With a Purpose™ courses.

Active learning leads students in doing things that help them understand important principles, messages, and ideas. It's a discovery process that helps kids internalize what they learn.

Research about active learning indicates that maximum

learning results when students are involved in direct, purposeful experiences. With that in mind, each Projects With a Purpose course gives teachers tools to facilitate some sort of project that results in direct, purposeful experiences for teenagers. Projects, experiences, and immersion into real-life faith action characterize this curriculum. In fact, you could probably call this the "project" curriculum since each course produces a tangible result. You'll find plenty of helpful hints that will make this course easy for you to teach and meaningful to your students.

Projects With a Purpose courses takes learning to a new level—giving teenagers an opportunity to discover something significant about their faith. And kids learn the important skills of working together, sharing one another's troubles, and supporting each other in love.

Projects With a Purpose courses offers a fun, alternative way for teenagers to put their faith into action. Use them to involve your kids in Christian growth experiences they'll remember for a lifetime.

Before the 4-Week Course

■ Read the Introduction, the Course Objectives, and This Course at a Glance.

■ Determine when you'll use this course. Projects With a Purpose works well in Sunday school classes, midweek meetings, home Bible studies, youth groups, special-interest groups, leadership groups, retreats, camps, or any time you want to help teenagers discover more about their faith.

■ Decide how you'll publicize the course using the clip art on the Publicity Page (p. 8). Prepare fliers, newsletter articles, and posters as needed.

■ Look at the Bonus Ideas (p. 38) and decide which ones you'll use.

Before Each Lesson

Read the opening statements, Objectives, and Bible Basis for the lesson. The Bible Basis focuses on a key biblical theme for the activity, experience, or Bible study portion of the lesson.

Gather necessary supplies from This Lesson at a Glance.

Read each section of the lesson. Adjust as necessary for your class size and meeting room.

Helpful Hints

■ The approximate minutes listed give you an idea of how long each activity will take. Each lesson in a Projects With a Purpose course is designed to fill an hour-long time slot. Some lessons may require work outside of class, depending on the project for the course. You might also consider restructuring your class time, if possible, to allow more time to complete projects.

The answers given after discussion questions are responses your students *might* give. They aren't the only answers or the "right" answers. If needed, use them to spark discussion. Kids won't always say what you wish they'd say. That's why some of the responses given are negative or controversial. If someone responds negatively, don't be shocked. Accept the person and use the opportunity to explore other angles of the issue.

■ If you see you're going to have extra time, do an activity or two from the "If You Still Have Time..." section at the end of each lesson or from the Bonus Ideas (p. 38).

■ Dive into the activities with the kids. Don't be a spectator. The experience will be more successful and rewarding for both you and your students when you play an active role.

■ Have fun with the lessons as you lead your teenagers. Remember, it was Jesus who encouraged us to become "like little children." Besides, how often do your kids get *permission* to express their childlike qualities?

■ Be prepared for surprises. In Projects With a Purpose courses, you don't always know which way the lesson will go. Much of your job will be directing kids to stay on task, rather than leading specific activities. As facilitator, you'll be helping kids make their own faith discoveries rather than directing the results of a specific activity.

■ Encourage new leaders to participate in teaching this course. Projects With a Purpose offers an exciting way to give new volunteers a hands-on look at the positive impact youth ministry can have on teenagers.

■ Rely on the Holy Spirit to help you. Remember, only God can give true spiritual insight. Concentrate on your role as the facilitator and trust the Holy Spirit to work in the hearts of your kids.

You Can Do It!

Because Projects With a Purpose courses are a different approach to Christian education, leading the lessons might seem a bit scary at first.

That's OK. In fact, it's normal to be a little nervous about a new teaching method. Innovation often requires a risk for the teacher. But hang in there. With the Holy Spirit's guidance and your own desire to make these lessons succeed, great things will happen in your kids' lives.

PUBLICITY PAGE

Grab your students' attention! Photocopy this page, then cut out and paste the clip art of your choice in your church bulletin or newsletter to advertise this course on prayer. Or photocopy and use the ready-made flier as a bulletin insert. Permission to photocopy this clip art is granted for local church use.

Splash the clip art on posters, fliers, or even postcards! Just add the vital details: the date and time the course begins and where you'll meet.

It's that simple.

A 4-week project to help teenagers discover how prayer can change their lives

Come to ....

On ....

At ....

Come experience what real prayer can do!

What Is Prayer?

People often view prayer as an impossible task—a mysterious, mist-covered cosmic link between God and a select few highly spiritual people. But ask anyone who's faced a life-threatening emergency, and that person will know exactly what prayer is—talking to God. What seems to be so difficult to do in ordinary life can easily become as natural as breathing when danger threatens us or someone we love.

This lesson will help students bridge the "danger gap" and discover how prayer can be a normal focus of everyday life.

LESSON AIM

Students will learn how to pray more effectively and create their own prayer journal.

OBJECTIVES

Students will
- experience hindrances to prayer,
- discover the parts of prayer,
- create a personal prayer journal, and
- learn about the purpose of this course.

BIBLE BASIS

PHILIPPIANS 4:6-7
JAMES 5:13-18

Look up the following key Bible passages. Then read the background paragraphs to see how the passages relate to your students. These Scriptures will be explored during the Bible study portion of this lesson.

Philippians 4:6-7 instructs Christians how to pray and avoid worry.

Paul wrote this letter to the Philippians while he was in prison, so his encouragement to pray and not worry didn't come from abstract theological beliefs. Paul lived what he wrote. He knew that the secret to peace and freedom from worry was an active, daily prayer life with God.

The same truth Paul learned in prison applies to Christians today. Many would argue that the number and depth of today's worries far exceed those of Paul's times—especially for young people. But whether kids are faced with drugs, gang violence, divorce, or the more ordinary worries of relationships, acceptance, and school, they can take Paul's lesson to heart and find relief in their own lives.

James 5:13-18 gives Christians instructions on prayer.

In this passage, James outlines many of prayer's applications in Christians' daily lives. He instructs Christians to pray in all kinds of circumstances—trouble, happiness, sickness, or even when we've sinned. James knew that prayer is our lifeline to God, and there is no situation in life in which prayer isn't needed.

Most people today pray only when tragedy strikes or when bad times come unexpectedly. But Christians need to understand that prayer is much more than a spiritual version of *Rescue 911*. Prayer is our primary way of communicating with God, the source of our life (Colossians 3:1-3). As students discover that prayer isn't just an emergency line to God, they can be free to explore how prayer can saturate their entire lives.

THIS LESSON AT A GLANCE

Section	Minutes	What Students Will Do	Supplies
Introduction	up to 10	**Talk Trouble**—Define the purpose of this course and tell about a favorite hobby or experience.	
Bible Study	up to 25	**Prayer P.A.R.T.S.**—Discuss the various parts of a healthy prayer life.	Bibles, "P.A.R.T.S. of Prayer" handouts (p. 15)
Project Work	up to 25	**Prayer Journal**—Create a personal prayer journal.	Newsprint, markers, small notebooks, tape, "P.A.R.T.S. of Prayer" handouts (p. 15), "Journal Guide One" handouts (p. 16), pencils
	up to 10	**Prayer Connections**—Commit to pray for a partner during the coming week.	Prayer journals from the "Prayer Journal" activity, pencils
Closing	up to 5	**Prayer Song**—Sing "Psalm 5" to God.	Bibles

The Lesson

INTRODUCTION

Talk Trouble
(up to 10 minutes)

Welcome students to the class. Say: **Today we're going to begin a four-week exploration of prayer. But instead of typical activities and discussions, we're going to actually experience many different kinds of prayer and discover how to practice each of them more effectively in our lives.**

Open with prayer. Then have kids pair up to tell each other about a favorite hobby or fun experience from the past. Explain that as each person shares, he or she must say the other person's name after every sentence or phrase spoken. For example, "Karen, I like to whittle, Karen, because, Karen, it makes me feel peaceful. And, Karen, it allows me time to just think, Karen, about whatever I want."

After a few minutes call everyone back together. Then have kids repeat to the class what their partners told them, only this time instruct kids to speak in a medieval dialect. For example, "Bob hath told me that he doth like to whittle. He saith he liketh it because it bringeth him peace and provideth free time to pondereth life's mysteries."

After everyone has shared, say: **You've just experienced two common ways of praying that are awkward and often make prayer more difficult. Today we're going to explore much more about prayer and learn how we can make prayer more than speaking in a specific way. We're going to explore how to make prayer simple and meaningful for each of us.**

Prayer P.A.R.T.S.
(up to 25 minutes)

Say: **Before we start exploring how to build up our personal prayer lives, let's look at the parts that make up a healthy prayer life.**

Form five groups. Give students each a copy of the "P.A.R.T.S. of Prayer" handout (p. 15) and assign each group one of the five parts of prayer listed on the handout. Make sure kids have Bibles so they can look up the passages listed at the top of the handout. Tell each group to read the passages and decide how their assigned part could be practically and simply expressed in real life. Ask groups each to come up with a creative way to teach the class how to apply their part to everyday life. For example, groups might perform a skit, teach a song, or play a game to pass on their information.

When groups are ready have them teach their prayer parts to the rest of the class. When you've covered all the parts, form new groups of no more than five by mixing up people from the different P.A.R.T.S. groups. Ask the following questions one at a time and allow groups to discuss them. Then have volunteers from each group share their insights with the class. Ask:

■ **What's the most important part of prayer? Explain.** (Praise, because it focuses us on God; they're all equally important.)

■ **What part of prayer is easiest for you? Explain.** (Asking for things, because I'm selfish; sharing with God, because I like having someone to talk to.)

■ **What's the hardest part of prayer? Explain.** (Praise, because I can't think of anything to say; asking for things, because I feel like I'm taking up too much of God's time.)

■ **How is the variety of ways people teach us about prayer like the variety of ways people pray?** (Some people use singing as prayer; some people are quiet about prayer; some people really get into prayer and others do it because they feel they have to.)

■ **Why don't people pray all the time?** (Because they don't know what to say; because they're ashamed of how they live.)

■ **Why is it important for Christians to pray?** (Because prayer is how we learn to follow God; because it's how we get to know God.)

■ **What keeps you from praying?** (Laziness; other problems in my life; fear of God's punishment when I sin.)

■ **How can you begin to overcome these hindrances?** (I can take my problems to God; I can accept the truth that God will forgive my sins.)

Say: **Prayer isn't always easy, even for mature Christians. But when we put all the parts together, we can see that it is simple—so simple that anyone can do it. Let's explore how we can start practicing prayer in our lives so we can know God better.**

PROJECT WORK

Prayer Journal
(up to 25 minutes)

Tape three sheets of newsprint on the wall and write one of these titles on each sheet:
■ Sheet 1: "Things I Like to Do By Myself"
■ Sheet 2: "Things I Like to Do With a Few People"
■ Sheet 3: "Things I Like to Do With a Big Crowd"

Provide markers and have kids each write one appropriate response on each sheet of newsprint.

After several people have explained what they wrote, say: **Over the next four weeks we're going to explore how prayer can be a dynamic part of life in these three contexts. Today we're going to begin this exploration by creating a personal prayer journal and learning how to use one in daily life. Prayer journals not only keep track of your conversations with God, they also provide a way for you to see how God is working in your life over a period of time and help you keep your life focused on God.**

Distribute small notebooks, tape, and markers. Have students decorate their prayer journals. While they're decorating instruct kids each to tape their "P.A.R.T.S. of Prayer" handout on the inside front cover of their journal.

Once students have decorated their journals, distribute the "Journal Guide One" handouts (p. 16) and pencils. Have students form pairs to complete the handout. (The handout will help kids explore their feelings about praying alone, with a small group, or in a big crowd.)

When pairs are finished, form new groups of no more than six and have kids respond in their groups to these questions:
■ **Are you nervous about praying alone? Why or why not?**
■ **How do you feel about praying aloud?**
■ **What's your biggest fear when it comes to prayer?**

As a closing for this part of the lesson, have group members tell each person one quality they see in that person that would help him or her be effective in prayer. For example, "You have a lot of compassion for others" or "You're always sincere in what you say." Have group members pray aloud for each other that God will help them overcome their fears concerning prayer.

Prayer Connections

(up to 10 minutes)

Have kids form new pairs. In their journals have kids create a request/answer column similar to the one in the box in the margin.

Have students write in today's date, then list up to three personal prayer requests under the request column. Suggest that these prayers be something they would feel comfortable sharing with someone else. Have kids then copy their partners' lists into their own request columns. Ask kids to commit to praying each day this week for their partners' requests as well as their own.

During the next week encourage young people to write out their prayers. If some of your class members don't feel comfortable doing this, ask them instead to write out a brief summary of each prayer time by writing the date along with answers to these questions:
- What did you talk with God about?
- What did God tell you, if anything?
- How did you feel after praying?

Ask kids who choose this option to write these questions in their journals for future reference.

Table Talk

The "Table Talk" activity in this course helps teenagers explore with their parents what it means to share their faith with others. If you choose to use the "Table Talk" activity, this is a good time to show students the "Table Talk" handout (p. 17). Ask them to spend time with their parents completing it.

Before kids leave, give them each the "Table Talk" handout to take home or tell them you'll be sending it to their parents. Tell kids to be prepared to report next week on their experiences with the handout.

Request/Answer Prayer Sheet Sample

Date	Request	Date	Answer

Teacher Tip

Students may wonder how they'll know if their prayers have been answered. Remind teenagers that we don't always get the answer we're hoping for or expecting but that God does answer prayer. Encourage kids to look beyond the obvious when trying to determine if a prayer has been answered. Also have teenagers talk with friends to get new insights about answered prayers.

Teacher Tip

If kids don't know how to get started in prayer this week, remind them of the "P.A.R.T.S. of Prayer" guide in their journals. The parts are in no particular order, but encourage kids to try to include each element in their prayers this week.

Prayer Song

(up to 5 minutes)

Say: **We've explored today how prayer can be conveyed in silence, in speech, or in writing. Let's close today by praying in one form we haven't talked about—song.**

Have students form a circle and join hands. Lead the group in singing "Psalm 5" (or another chorus that deals with prayer). After the prayer remind kids to pray each day for their personal requests and their partners' requests. Tell students to bring their prayer journals next week when they will rejoin their partners to discuss how God has answered their prayers.

If You Still Have Time . . .

Prayer Song—Distribute Bibles, paper, and pencils, and have kids turn a psalm into a personal prayer to God by paraphrasing it based on their own circumstances. Some good psalms to use include Psalm 23; 25; 27; 32; 51; 64; and 84.

Focus on P.A.R.T.S.—Have kids choose one part of prayer from the "P.A.R.T.S. of Prayer" handout (p. 15) and spend the remaining time practicing that part of prayer together. For example, if students choose "praise," then have kids take turns speaking wonderful truths about God's goodness. Close the prayer by singing a praise chorus or hymn.

P.A.R.T.S. OF PRAYER

Read the following Scripture passages and decide how your assigned part of prayer can be effectively and simply lived out in daily life. Then come up with a creative way to teach what you've learned to the rest of the class.

Scripture passages: Philippians 4:6-7 and James 5:13-18.

Praise

Praising God simply means telling God things that are true about him. Praising brings God pleasure and helps us keep our focus on the truth about God's nature and love for us.

Ask

Asking means letting God know about your needs and desires, as well as the needs and desires of those you care about. It's perfectly fine to ask God for things, even if they're things we know we don't need. But it's equally important to remember that God's answer to any request may be "wait" or "no."

Repent

Repenting means telling God whenever there's sin in your life and actively choosing to turn away from it immediately, with no intention of doing it again.

Thank

Prayers of thanks tell God about all the things you're grateful for in life.

Share

Sharing means talking with God like you would a close friend. Unlike many people's opinion of God as a "distant, stuck-up, uninterested king," the real God is humble and loving—and all-powerful, too. God wants to hear about what happens to you each day. And God's power can give you strength for the little struggles you face each day as well as the big challenges.

In your prayer journal write answers to the following questions:

■ What's your biggest struggle when it comes to praying alone?

■ If you spend time praying alone with God every day, what do you get out of it? If you don't spend time alone in prayer each day, write down what you think you'd get out of it.

■ What's your biggest struggle when it comes to praying in front of other people?

■ If it were impossible for you to feel nervous or afraid, do you think you'd enjoy praying with other people? Why or why not?

■ What good could come from praying with your friends on a regular basis?

■ What's one thing you can do to overcome fears you have about praying with a group of people?

■ How can you help other people overcome their fears of praying with a group?

Table Talk

To the Parent: We're involved in a four-week course at church called *Teaching Teenagers to Pray.* Students are exploring how to develop prayer as a dynamic focus in their lives. We'd like you and your teenager to spend some time discussing how prayer has affected your life. Use this "Table Talk" page to help you do that.

Parent

- When in your life did prayer mean the most to you? Explain.
- Is prayer important to you now? Why or why not?
- What do you think prayer accomplishes in a person's life?
- What effect does prayer have on God?

Teenager

- What do you pray about the most?
- What do you wish you knew about prayer that you don't know now?
- Who has had a significant role in helping you develop your prayer life?

Parent and teenager

- Does your family pray together regularly? Why or why not?
- Would you like your family to pray with you more often? Why or why not?
- What would you like to pray about with your family?
- Read Ephesians 3:14-19 together. How might this prayer be adapted to fit your family?

In the space below, rewrite Ephesians 3:14-19 to create a family prayer. Each day this week, gather as a family to pray this prayer and to pray for any other family members' needs. If you don't already have a weekly family prayer time, consider starting one beginning next week.

Private Prayer

Most young Christians who struggle with prayer talk about their uneasiness with praying out loud with others. Sometimes that's just shyness, but it can also be an indication of a Christian's private struggles with prayer. This lesson focuses on prayer that happens—or doesn't happen—when no one else is looking.

LESSON AIM

Students will learn how to pray alone and plan a private prayer time with God.

OBJECTIVES

Students will
■ discuss how private prayer helps them,
■ explore the struggles that come with praying alone, and
■ design a private prayer getaway with God.

BIBLE BASIS

MATTHEW 14:23
MARK 1:35
LUKE 5:16; 6:12-13

Look up the following key Bible passages. Then read the background paragraphs to see how the passages relate to your students. These Scriptures will be explored during the Bible study portion of this lesson.

Matthew 14:23; Mark 1:35; and **Luke 5:16; 6:12-13** all speak of times when Jesus went off alone to pray.

Each of the four gospel accounts describes what Jesus did during much of his life on earth. His teachings, healings, confrontations—all of the things that involved other people—are recorded in detail. With all that activity it's often easy to overlook the things Jesus did that aren't recorded in detail; for example, his private prayer life. No one knows what went on during those private times. But Jesus seemed to spend a lot of time alone with God. And if Jesus needed to pray, so do we.

For most people prayer is difficult to define. People who have little experience with prayer often compare it to practices they can more readily imagine—such as meditation, giving a speech, or invoking a spell. But until Christians can become familiar with the true nature of prayer and grow comfortable walking in prayer as a lifestyle, their Christianity will be flavorless—void of real life and power. By looking closely at the priority Jesus placed on private prayer, young people can come to understand not only the nature of true prayer but the role private prayer can play in their lives.

Section	Minutes	What Students Will Do	Supplies
Introduction	up to 10	**Prayer Relief**—Call out why people pray and how prayer helps them.	Newsprint, marker
Bible Study	up to 15	**Threading the Needle**—Try to thread a needle while being harassed.	Needles, thread, Bibles
Project Work	up to 20	**Prayer Excursion**—Design a private prayer excursion with God.	"Journal Guide Two" handouts (pp. 23-24), pencils, prayer journals from lesson 1, tape
	up to 10	**Up Next**—Learn about next week's project.	Newsprint, markers
Closing	up to 5	**Excursion Partners**—Commit to praying for each other this week.	Pencils, prayer journals from lesson 1

The Lesson

Prayer Relief

(up to 10 minutes)

Have prayer partners from last week get together to talk about answers to prayer that may have come during the week. Have kids update their journals.

Open with prayer. Welcome guests and visitors. Have a class member explain to guests what the class is working on.

Say: **Today we're going to explore together the mysterious realm called private prayer. Let's begin by calling out why people pray and how prayer helps them.**

List kids' responses on a sheet of newsprint. After several reasons have been listed, ask:

■ **Why are there so many different reasons people pray alone?** (Everyone has different needs; some people rely solely on private prayer.)

Say: **There certainly are a lot of good reasons we should spend time alone in prayer. Now let's explore why private prayer is so often a struggle for Christians.**

INTRODUCTION

Teacher Tip

Remind kids that God answers all our prayers, but God's answers aren't always what we expect or want. God can say no or wait just as often as yes.

BIBLE STUDY

Threading the Needle

(up to 15 minutes)

Form groups of four. Give one person in each group a needle and thread. On "go," have the person holding the needle try to thread it while the rest of the group tries to stop him or her without touching that person. Tell group members they can blow the thread, jump around, yell, talk, make faces—anything to distract the person short of touching him or her. Allow time for each group member to try to thread the needle.

When groups are finished ask the following questions one at a time. Allow time for all group members to answer the questions, then have volunteers share their groups' responses with the class. Ask:

■ **Did you enjoy threading the needle? Why or why not?** (No, it was more trouble than it was worth; yes, I liked the challenge.)

■ **What's your reaction to all the forces trying to distract you from threading the needle?** (I tried to ignore them, but they kept invading my space; they made it impossible to hold the thread still.)

■ **How is this experience like trying to pray alone?** (I am easily distracted by the things around me; I have a hard time thinking of things to say.)

Have groups read aloud Matthew 14:23; Mark 1:35; and Luke 5:16; 6:12-13. Then have teenagers discuss the following questions in their groups, reporting insights back to the class when finished. Ask:

■ **Why did Jesus need to pray?** (I don't know; he needed to be strengthened by God just like we do; he needed God's direction in his life.)

■ **Why did Jesus go off alone to pray?** (So he wouldn't be distracted; so no one could find him.)

■ **What do you think Jesus talked with God about?** (He probably asked for God's strength; he asked God to show him what to do next.)

■ **As people who follow Christ, what can we learn from Jesus' example in these passages?** (That private prayer is important; that we should pray in places where we won't be disturbed; that we should pray all the time.)

Say: **One reason Jesus came to earth was to show us how to live the Christian life. If he needed to pray alone all the time,** so do we. Let's try a "spiritual growth" experiment to help us develop our private prayer lives.

Prayer Excursion
(up to 20 minutes)

Distribute pencils and the "Journal Guide Two" handouts (pp. 23-24). The handout provides an outline to help kids plan a private prayer excursion with God. Form groups of four and have group members work together to plan private excursions for each group member.

If students have any difficulty planning their private excursions, encourage them to scan the "Excursion Ideas" box on the handout. When everyone's plan is completed, have group members arrange a time toward the end of the week to get together and discuss their experiences. For example, suggest that group members get together for pizza or have a movie night at a group member's home. To help kids each remember the time and place of their group's meeting, encourage students to write the information on their handouts or on the back page of their prayer journals. Tell kids to use the "Post-Excursion Discussion Guide" box on the handout to help them share their prayer experiences.

When all the arrangements have been made, have students fold their handouts and tape them inside their prayer journals. Remind kids to take their journals with them when they meet with group members later in the week. Close the activity by praying together for God to bless the time kids will spend with him this week.

Up Next
(up to 10 minutes)

Say: **Before we close our time together today I want to give you a brief preview of next week.**

On a sheet of newsprint, write each of these special groups:
- "Hospital patients"
- "Children's hospital ward"
- "Elderly shut-ins"
- "Church leadership (pastors and teachers)"
- "Children's Sunday school class"
- "Church nursery"
- "Adult Sunday school class"

Say: **Next week we'll be going out in teams to pray for special groups of people. Since we can't pray for everyone on this list, let's vote to see which two or three groups we will visit.**

Go down the list and have students each give one vote for their favorite choice. Write kids' names next to their favorite choices. After the voting, pick out the two or three top choices and tell kids they will go and pray for their special group next week. (If any young people voted for a group that isn't in the top three, ask them to tell you which of the chosen groups they're willing to join. Then add their names to the list.)

PROJECT WORK

Teacher Tip

As groups are working on the private excursions, make sure students don't choose a location near another student (unless the excursions are on different days) and encourage kids to stay away from busy, distracting locations.

Teacher Tip

Remind kids to review the "P.A.R.T.S. of Prayer" handout in their journals as they're designing their prayer excursion this week.

Teacher Tip

If groups choose to pray for Sunday school classes or church leadership, and you aren't meeting during the regular Sunday school hour, make arrangements for kids to visit the classes on the Sunday before your next meeting.

CLOSING

Teacher Tip

Before your next meeting time, make arrangements for kids to meet with the special groups they've chosen. If your group has chosen to visit a hospital, contact the hospital's administrator to ask who might most enjoy the kids' visit. During that visit make sure kids know they must ask each person for permission before praying for him or her. If the person says no, have kids pray for that person when the visit is over.

Excursion Partners

(up to 5 minutes)

Say: **Let's close today's lesson by returning to our prayer-excursion planning groups.**

Once kids are back in their groups, have group members pair off and commit to praying for their partners during their prayer-excursion times. Have kids write in their journals the time of their partners' excursions as a reminder to pray for them. Also remind kids to bring their journals to class next week.

Then have groups close in prayer by forming circles, holding hands, and thanking God for one quality they appreciate about the person on their right.

If You Still Have Time...

Prayer Memories—Form a circle and ask students to share about a time when they felt God's presence in prayer. Discuss what makes those experiences different from other prayer times.

Journal Review—Have volunteers share their successes and struggles in using their prayer journals over the past week. Have kids offer suggestions for each other on how to make better use of their journals each day.

JOURNAL GUIDE TWO

Use this guide to help you plan your own private excursion with God this week.

To begin, choose a specific two-hour block of time that you can set aside this week for a prayer excursion:

_____

Next, think of all the safe, private places you know of where you can escape without being disturbed. Write those here:

Now choose one as your location for this week's prayer excursion:

_____

OK, now that you have the time and place, think about what you'll do during that time. Circle each of the activities below that you enjoy:

- ■ Writing   ■ Singing   ■ Sitting in silence   ■ Talking

- ■ Reading   ■ Drawing   ■ Walking/hiking

Now choose two or three activities to include in your excursion this week. For example, you could go on a short hike to a private place, then write a letter to God or draw a picture of how you feel.

Next, focus on what you want to talk about with God during your excursion. In the space below, write three things you're excited about in life right now followed by three things that are troubling you:

What sorts of questions would you like to ask God about these things? Write three or four questions below:

Finally, consider how God might speak to you. On your excursion you'll need a Bible with a concordance in the back. (If you're not sure how to use a concordance, ask your teacher to show you.) Based on the issues you want to talk about, use the concordance to find verses that relate to those topics. For example, if you're worried about a relationship that's in trouble, look in the concordance under "friend," "friendship," or "love." Write those Scripture references below:

Remember, on your excursion you'll need your prayer journal, this handout, and a Bible with a concordance. Congratulations! You're all set to go!

Excursion Ideas

- Go on a nature hike.
- Drive to a secluded part of the country near your community.
- Spend the time in your church's auditorium (if it's empty).
- Go to a park.
- Go into a well-ventilated closet.

Post-Excursion Discussion Guide

Ask your group members these questions to spark discussion:
- What did you do on your excursion?
- What did you learn about yourself on your excursion?
- What did you learn about God?
- How does God speak to you best? Explain.
- In what way are you most comfortable speaking to God? Explain.
- What disappointed you about your excursion?
- What did you like about it?
- Will you do it again? Why or why not?
- If you do another excursion, what will you do differently?

Team Prayer

T he thought of praying with other people out loud often brings shudders of fright and anxiety to young people. Kids are afraid of sounding foolish or fumbling with words. Their lack of confidence in praying aloud may stem from a lack of experience in praying alone or a general apprehension of sharing something as personal as prayer with a group of friends.

This lesson focuses on helping kids overcome their fears and provides a safe environment for them to experience genuine team prayer.

LESSON AIM

Students will learn how to pray together and go in teams to pray for others.

OBJECTIVES

Students will
- discuss things that make them feel uncomfortable,
- identify the importance of teamwork,
- plan a team prayer outing, and
- experience team prayer.

BIBLE BASIS

LUKE 9:18, 28
EPHESIANS 6:18

Look up the following key Bible passages. Then read the background paragraphs to see how the passages relate to your teenagers. These Scriptures will be explored during the Bible study portion of today's lesson.

Luke 9:18, 28 shows how Jesus related to his disciples through prayer.

Even though Jesus spent much of his time in prayer alone in the wilderness, he also prayed when he was with his disciples. From these two verses, we can see that Jesus felt comfortable praying with his disciples or just praying near them. Prayer was such an essential part of the daily routine that it was commonplace—though never common.

Many young people view prayer as an "emergency line." They don't realize their need to stay near God through prayer each day. Likewise, praying with others can seem as unnatural as trying to speak a foreign language. But Jesus and his disciples didn't see prayer that way. Teenagers need to learn from Jesus' example how they can make prayer a constant part of their lives.

Ephesians 6:18 instructs Christians to pray for each other.

As an apostle on the "front lines" of Christ's work, Paul understood the vital importance of having Christians pray for each other. The members of Christ's body were never meant to work in isolation, any more than the parts of our physical bodies are able to do so. Group prayer is a powerful connector that links Christians together and strengthens us to overcome.

In our Western culture of isolation, the idea of a unified body of believers may be hard for teenagers to grasp. But within each of them is the need to belong to a community. Group prayer can help build that community among teenagers and move God to act on behalf of those they pray for.

THIS LESSON AT A GLANCE

Section	Minutes	What Students Will Do	Supplies
Introduction	up to 5	**Comfort Zones**—Tell about things that make them feel uncomfortable.	
Bible Study	up to 15	**Getting It Across**—Try to get others to do something without speaking to them.	Bibles
Project Work	up to 30	**Team Prayer**—Go with a team to pray for a special group or person.	"Team-Prayer Guide" handouts (p. 30), pencils, prayer journals from lesson 1
	up to 10	**Up Next**—Make ad posters for next week's prayer event.	Poster board, art supplies
Closing	up to 5	**New Connections**—Find new prayer partners for the coming week.	Prayer journals from lesson 1, pencils

INTRODUCTION

Teacher Tip

As volunteers share, remind kids that it's OK if their prayer excursions weren't earth-shattering. Like any relationship, intimacy and feelings of closeness are developed over time.

The Lesson

Comfort Zones

(up to 5 minutes)

Open with prayer. Welcome guests and visitors. Have a class member explain to guests what the class has been working on in the past week. Invite volunteers to tell about their personal prayer excursions and about the debriefing time they had with friends later in the week.

Say: **Today we're going to move beyond private prayer into another kind of prayer that can be just as exciting and meaningful—praying with others. Before we begin let's form** a tight circle in the center of the room.

Once everyone is huddled together, have kids each call out something that makes them feel uncomfortable, such as taking a test or speaking in front of a large group. As each person calls out have kids take one step away from the center of the circle if they agree with the person who's speaking.

When the circle is totally destroyed, say: **Feeling uncomfortable can be a normal, healthy reaction to any kind of unfamiliar situation. For example, praying aloud with others can make many people feel uncomfortable because they aren't sure what they should say. Today we're going to help each other overcome our discomfort about group prayer and learn to pray together effectively.**

Getting It Across

(up to 15 minutes)

Say: **Let's begin our exploration of group prayer by doing a fun activity that requires teamwork.**

Form teams of four. Have one person from each team leave the room while the other three people on each team decide on an action they want their teammate to perform. For example, team members may choose to have their teammate remove his or her shoes and parade around the room wearing them as earrings.

When teams are ready, have the exiled team members return to the room and listen while you explain the activity. Then have teams each try to get their fourth person to perform the act they chose. Teams may make noises and gesture freely, but they may not talk or write at any time during the activity. Call time when most of the teams have gotten their fourth person to perform the act.

Gather everyone together and ask:

■ **What did you learn about teamwork from this activity?** (That we all had to agree on what our movements meant before we tried to show our fourth person; that it's not easy to have teamwork without clear communication.)

■ **What frustrated you most about this activity?** (Not being able to get my message across; not being understood by my teammates.)

■ **How is that frustration like the frustration that sometimes comes with group prayer?** (I don't know how to say what I'm feeling; I don't think anyone around me will understand me.)

Read aloud Luke 9:18, 28 and Ephesians 6:18. Then ask:

■ **If you had been one of the disciples would you have felt uncomfortable praying around Jesus? Why or why not?** (Yes, I would've felt like a grasshopper next to a giant; no, because he would understand my heart.)

■ **If the disciples did feel uncomfortable, why was it important that they overcome their fear?** (Because they needed the strength prayer could bring; because it was important to their ministry.)

Say: **Just as the disciples learned to make group prayer a** common part of their lives, we're also directed to pray for each other at all times. Let's follow the disciples' example and form teams for prayer.

Team Prayer
(up to 30 minutes)

Have students form the prayer groups they voted to be a part of last week. If you have new people this week, have them join the group of their choice. Allow visitors to be "silent partners" unless they want to pray aloud.

Distribute a pencil and a "Team-Prayer Guide" handout (p. 30) to each person. The handout will help groups decide how they'll approach their prayer situations. When groups have each completed their handout, read it yourself to make sure kids are on target, then send them off to their prayer destinations. Make sure kids understand they need to return to the classroom within 30 minutes.

When kids return from their prayer trips, have them discuss the following questions in their groups. Then have volunteers from each group share their groups' insights with the class. Ask:
- **What's your reaction to this experience?**
- **What was the response of the people you prayed for?**
- **How do you feel about what you did? Explain.**
- **What's one thing you'll do differently next time? Explain.**

After hearing from volunteers, say: **Praying as a team can be exciting, and it's a great way to build community and show love to others. Now let's talk about what happens when lots of teams of people join together in a "concert" of prayer.**

Have kids stay in the same groups for the next activity.

Up Next
(up to 10 minutes)

Briefly describe to class members what they'll be working on next week (see "This Lesson at a Glance" for lesson 4, page 32). Distribute poster board and art supplies to each group and instruct group members to work together to create a poster advertising next week's Concert of Prayer. Make sure the posters indicate that the concert will take place during the regular worship service.

When groups are finished collect the posters and ask for volunteers to help you hang them around the church after class.

New Connections
(up to 5 minutes)

Have students find new prayer partners and share prayer requests for this week. Have partners write their requests in the request/answer section of their prayer journals and commit to praying for each other every day this week.

PROJECT WORK

Teacher Tip

If kids are going off church grounds, provide the needed number of adult drivers. Also, if kids are going to another class, send along an adult volunteer to make sure things go smoothly.

Teacher Tip

Make arrangements with the pastor to use 10 to 15 minutes of the worship service next week. For example, the concert could take the place of the regular music next week.

CLOSING

When pairs are finished, close the meeting by having kids each write in their partner's journal one positive quality they've discovered about that person during this course. Remind kids to bring their journals to class next week.

If You Still Have Time...

Concert Announcement—In addition to the posters have students create a short drama to advertise the prayer concert next week. Have kids perform the drama during the regular announcement time in today's service.

Team-Prayer Share—Have teams from today's prayer activity share their experiences with the other teams in the class. Then form new teams of volunteers who are willing to get together during the coming week and pray for whatever is on their hearts. Have teams report back to the class next week on their prayer time.

TEAM-PRAYER GUIDE

Answer the questions below to help your team decide how it will approach your special prayer time today.

1. How will you position yourselves when you pray together? Will you

   ■ stand?
   ■ sit?
   ■ hold hands?
   ■ surround the group you're praying for?
   ■ place your hands on their shoulders?
   ■ stand off to one side?

2. Who will pray?

3. Will you pray in any particular order or at random?

4. Who will start the prayer? end it?

5. What will you pray for?

6. Will you ask the people you're praying for to provide prayer requests before you pray? If so, how will you make sure everyone's request gets prayed for?

7. How will you include all the "parts" in your prayer? (See the "P.A.R.T.S. of Prayer" sheet in your prayer journal.)

8. What will you do after the prayer to say thanks to the people for letting you pray for them?

Corporate Prayer

Few things in Christian life are as powerful as an entire church body united in prayer. Sadly, such "bodywide" encounters with God are rare in the Western church. Severe illness, death, or other unexpected tragedies are often the only motivators that can still bring a body of believers together in focused prayer.

This lesson gives young people the opportunity to experience the power of united corporate prayer by guiding them in orchestrating a prayer concert with the congregation.

LESSON AIM

Students will learn about corporate prayer and design a concert of prayer for the congregation.

OBJECTIVES

Students will
- talk about answers to prayer they've had during the course,
- discover the importance of unity,
- design a prayer concert for the congregation, and
- lead the congregation in a concert of prayer.

BIBLE BASIS

JOHN 17:20-23
ACTS 2:42-47

Look up the following key Bible passages. Then read the background paragraphs to see how these passages relate to your teenagers. These Scriptures will be explored during the Bible study portion of this lesson.

In **John 17:20-23**, Jesus prays for his church.

In his final hours before death, Jesus poured out his heart before the Father. Jesus prayed not just for the disciples who followed him then but also for all the disciples who would follow later. He prayed for us. That prayer could have focused on any number of pivotal issues he knew would face the church—but Jesus chose rather to focus only on one. Unity. He knew that without complete unity the church could never show the world his gospel of truth (verse 23). Above all else, unity was Jesus' first concern.

Unity in Christ should also be the first concern of Christians in your church—including the young people. But what does unity mean to a class full of me-generation kids who have been raised on the motto from Judges 21:25, "Everyone did what was right in his own eyes"? Despite how today's teenagers were raised, they all have a need for unity with others. Through this lesson they will discover how corporate prayer can be a powerful tool for building that unity in Christ.

Acts 2:42-47 describes the practices of the first-century church.

The message of the gospel was fresh in the minds and hearts of the first-century believers. Many of them had seen Jesus in the flesh long before they came to believe in him. They had seen the way Jesus lived; they knew what he was like. Committing to live like him was more than a far-off dream for these people. It was a present reality. That's why it's important to recognize the priorities these "fresh" Christians set in their lives and the activities they considered vital to their victory as Christians. This passage lists only four such priorities. And one of the four is prayer.

Private prayer is important. But young people need to understand that not all prayer was meant to happen in a vacuum. As Christians we're called to live and function as a united body of believers. According to this passage we can help meet that goal by devoting ourselves to prayer—not just private prayer but united corporate prayer. Corporate prayer is one element in the glue that binds us together in Christ.

THIS LESSON AT A GLANCE

Section	Minutes	What Students Will Do	Supplies
Introduction	up to 10	**Answered Prayers**—Tell how their prayers have been answered over the past three weeks.	Prayer journals from lesson 1, pencils
Bible Study	up to 10	**United Creations**—Perform a task that requires a united effort.	Newsprint, markers, tape, scissors, Bibles
Project Work	up to 30	**Concert of Prayer**—Design a prayer concert for the congregation.	"Concert-Preparation Guide" handouts (pp. 36-37), pencils, name tags, markers
	up to 10	**Where We've Come From**—Discuss how they've grown since the course began.	Prayer journals from lesson 1, pencils
Closing	up to 5	**Preparation Prayer**—Pray together for God's blessing on the prayer concert.	

The Lesson

INTRODUCTION

Answered Prayers

(up to 10 minutes)

As kids arrive, have prayer partners from last week get together and share answers to prayer they may have received during the week. Have kids each update their prayer journals.

Open with prayer. Welcome guests and visitors. Have a class member explain to guests what the class is working on today. Then say: **Since today is the final week of our study on prayer, let's begin by talking about how God has answered your prayers over the past three weeks.**

Have volunteers share how God has answered some of their prayers. Let kids know it's OK to share negative as well as positive experiences. Remind kids that God answers prayer in ways we can't always understand or don't always agree with.

Once several students have shared, say: **During this course we've all experienced how prayer builds unity between us and God. This week we're going to discover how it can also build unity within Christ's body.**

United Creations

(up to 10 minutes)

Say: **To begin our exploration of how prayer can build unity in the church, let's have a race that can help us understand unity better.**

Form teams of three. Give each person on each team one of the following items: a set of markers, a pair of scissors, and a roll of tape. Give each team a large sheet of newsprint. Explain that the teams are to create something using all of the supplies. The item can be anything as long as it uses all the supplies and is easily recognizable by the other teams.

For the contest there are only two team rules:

■ no team member may use another team member's supplies and

■ team members may not talk or write to each other during the race.

Tell kids they'll have only three minutes to make their creations. Then start the race. During the race make sure no team members talk to each other or use each other's supplies.

Call time and have teams guess each other's creations. Then have teams explain their creations. Ask:

■ **What was difficult about this game?** (Trying to read each other's minds to figure out what we were trying to create; working together without talking.)

■ **How is this experience like what happens when you don't have unity with others?** (You don't let other people be themselves; you aren't all working to create the same thing.)

■ **What does it mean to have unity as Christians?** (That we love each other; that we accept each other and work together for a common purpose.)

Have a volunteer read John 17:20-23 and Acts 2:42-47. Ask:

■ **What do these passages say about unity?** (That it's very important to Jesus; that it takes work.)

■ **Based on these passages, what role does praying together play in building unity?** (When we pray together, we become more unified; without prayer we can't have unity.)

BIBLE STUDY

Say: **Today we're going to experience praying together on a large scale. In an effort to build unity in our church, we're going to create a concert of prayer and present it to our congregation today.**

Concert of Prayer
(up to 30 minutes)

Form a circle and distribute copies of the "Concert-Preparation Guide" handout (pp. 36-37). The handout will guide the class in planning the details of the prayer concert. Once kids have read the handout, lead them in forming groups according to interest as the handout suggests.

Once groups have completed the handout, walk through the process with the class and have representatives from each group explain to you the part they'll play in the concert. When you're satisfied that all the young people understand their roles, move on to the next activity.

Where We've Come From
(up to 10 minutes)

Say: **Before we close today's meeting and prepare for the prayer concert, let's take a few minutes to talk about how our attitudes toward prayer have changed over the past three weeks.**

Ask volunteers to share how their attitudes toward private or group prayer have changed since the course began. Once several people have shared, have kids form a circle and write in everyone's prayer journal one way they've seen each person grow during the course.

Say: **Even though the course is officially ending today, I encourage you to continue using your prayer journal regularly to record your prayers, requests, and God's answers. Also consider making group prayer a regular part of your week by forming permanent prayer partners or prayer groups when the class is over.**

Preparation Prayer
(up to 5 minutes)

Say: **As we get ready to set up our concert of prayer for the congregation, let's first prepare our hearts and ask for God's blessing.**

While kids are still in the circle, have them join hands in prayer. Allow several people to pray aloud at random before you close the prayer time. When the prayer is over, have kids review their prayer concert roles. Then go and enjoy the prayer concert together with the whole congregation.

To help your church benefit from the exciting prayer answers

PROJECT WORK

CLOSING

kids may have received during this course, encourage teenagers to write short articles based on their prayer journals to be included in your church newsletter or bulletin. Consider making this a regular feature in your newsletter or bulletin.

If You Still Have Time...

Permanent Prayer Connections—Have students form permanent prayer partnerships or groups and arrange times to meet regularly each week. Keep a record of these prayer groups so you can ask how they're doing in the weeks to come.

Sum It Up—Ask kids to respond to this question: "If you had to sum up in one sentence what you've learned in this course, what would you say?"

Teacher Tip

Before the service review the concert program with your pastor and see if you need to make any modifications.

Don't forget to provide the sound technician with the appropriate background music for the concert. Quiet instrumental music works best.

CONCERT-PREPARATION GUIDE

Use this sheet as a guide to help you and your class members design a concert of prayer for your congregation.

For the concert, there are three important roles. They are the
- prayer directors,
- section leaders, and
- solo artists.

The **prayer directors** job is to guide the overall direction of the concert by directing the congregation when to move from one topic to another.

The **section leaders** job is to listen to the prayer directors, then guide their sections in following the prayer directors' instructions.

The **solo artists** job is to listen to the section leaders and lead in prayer according to the topics their section leaders call out.

BEFORE GOING ON, DECIDE WHICH ROLE YOU'D LIKE THE MOST AND GATHER WITH OTHERS WHO'VE MADE THE SAME CHOICE.

1. Once you're all in clusters, work with other groups to create a floor-plan sketch of the church worship area. Carefully reproduce that sketch here:

2. Now divide the floor plan into sections according to the number of section leaders you have. (Make sure the sections are small enough so that each section leader will have no more than 30 people in his or her section.) Assign a section leader to each section.

For each section leader, assign one or more solo artists. Write the name of your section leader and solo artist(s) here:

3. Now join with the class in deciding what topics, issues, and concerns you'd like to lead the church in praying about. Assign one topic or concern to each prayer director. If you have less than five prayer directors, assign more than one topic to each person.

Write the names of your prayer directors and their assigned topics here:

INSTRUCTIONS

Once your teacher or pastor has explained the prayer concert to the congregation and divided the people according to sections, the section leaders and solo artists will move into their assigned sections of the worship area. The prayer directors will join the teacher or pastor up front.

Once the concert begins, the first prayer director will call out the first prayer topic for the congregation. The section leaders will then repeat the topic for their section and ask for specific prayer concerns relating to that topic. Then the solo artist will begin the prayer time by offering the first prayer. After others have prayed, the solo artist closes the prayer time.

After a few minutes the next prayer director will announce the next prayer topic or concern. As before, the section leaders and solo artists will guide their sections in following the prayer director's instructions.

The concert will be closed by a prayer from the pastor or an acappella song by the congregation, such as "Amazing Grace."

Here's an example of a prayer concert to help you get started.
1. The prayer director tells the whole congregation to pray about people who are hospitalized or sick.

2. Section leaders ask their sections for specific concerns relating to people who are sick, people who've been through medical traumas, and people who are fighting illness. Members of the section identify these people briefly. (It's the section leader's job to keep things moving.)

3. The solo artist opens the prayer time for his or her section by praying in general for the topic (and specifically for any other concerns). Then the rest of the section members may pray aloud for specifically mentioned requests. After an appropriate amount of time (agreed upon before the concert by your class), the solo artist will close the prayer.

4. A new prayer director introduces a new topic, such as poverty, homelessness, government, future church direction, family, spiritual growth, and so on. Then the process is repeated. This continues until all topics have been addressed in prayer.

That's it. Now create and put on your name tag, and you'll be ready for a real concert experience!

Bonus Ideas

MEETINGS AND MORE

Bonus Scriptures—The lessons focus on a select few Scripture passages, but if you'd like to incorporate more Bible readings into a lesson, here are some suggestions:
- 2 Chronicles 7:14 (God tells how prayer impacts his heart.)
- Matthew 21:18-22 (Jesus talks about the prayer of faith.)
- Luke 11:1-13 (Jesus teaches on prayer.)
- Romans 8:22-27 (Paul tells how the Holy Spirit helps us pray.)
- 1 Timothy 2:1 (Paul instructs Timothy on prayer in the church.)

After-Concert Lunch—After the final concert of prayer in lesson 4, gather kids together for lunch to debrief the experience. Ask students what they liked about the prayer concert and what questions or concerns it brought up. Pray together for God to use the experience to strengthen kids' prayer lives.

Prayer-Request Board—Set up a bulletin board in the meeting room for kids to post their prayer requests. Allow requests to be anonymous or signed. Encourage students to check the board frequently. Mark all answered prayers by drawing a red heart over the request.

School Prayer Group—Help teenagers who are interested organize a school-time prayer group. Check with the local school administration to see whether kids need to find a Christian teacher to sponsor the group. Using the "P.A.R.T.S. of Prayer" handout (p. 15) in their journals, have teenagers take turns leading weekly prayer times for interested students.

Concert Road Tour—As a way to build church unity, have your students sponsor more concerts of prayer for your congregation. Have each concert focus on a different theme, such as understanding of and love for those different from us, homelessness, or the problems of violence in America.

Once kids become confident in their leading abilities, take the concert of prayer on the road to other area churches. Kids can sponsor prayer concerts for other youth groups, Sunday school classes, or congregations. Over time you may even consider organizing a citywide concert of prayer in which several different prayer styles and denominations are represented.

Prayer-Journal Checkups—Have teenagers continue updating their prayer journals over the next 12 months. Encourage kids to write prayers about events in their lives that impact their faith. And encourage them to keep track of requests and answers to their prayers.

Meet once a month with kids who are keeping the journals to discuss journal entries and to pray together.

Different Prayer Styles—Take teenagers on a tour of area churches to have them observe worship services and interview church members about their prayer styles. Meet after each church visit to discuss the things learned about that denomination's prayer practices. Focus on the positives and look for prayer ideas you can incorporate into your church.

Famous Prayers—Have groups of no more than three visit a church library (or public library) to look for books about prayer or famous prayers. Many church leaders have had their prayers recorded in books of prayers. And written prayers are especially important to members of the Catholic community. Have groups study a few prayers and report their findings to the class.

Unity Tournament—Have kids organize a unique day of unity-building sporting events for your church. Have church members form teams of eight to 10 for tournaments of active sports, such as beach-ball volleyball, soccer, and foot races. For each game have team members tied together in a "bundle" formation to play. The team that acts with the most unity of movement and purpose will win.

After the event discuss how prayer builds unity in a church. And don't forget to close the event in prayer.

Weekend Concert of Prayer—Take the prayer-concert idea from lesson 4 and extend it over a full weekend of prayer events in a retreat setting. During the retreat lead kids in a variety of prayer expressions, such as praying through song, drawing, speaking, writing, dancing, and even playing.

Focus on Scriptures that give examples of various expressions of prayer. By exploring the variety of prayer, kids will begin to feel comfortable exploring new ways to express their prayers to God.

Make it a goal of the weekend to have kids each participate in at least five different prayer experiences.

PARTY PLEASER

RETREAT IDEA

CURRICULUM REORDER—TOP PRIORITY

Order now to prepare for your upcoming Sunday school classes, youth ministry meetings, and weekend retreats! Each book includes all teacher and student materials—plus photocopiable handouts—for any size class!

FOR JUNIOR HIGH/MIDDLE SCHOOL:

Accepting Others: Beyond Barriers & Stereotypes
ISBN 1-55945-126-2

Advice to Young Christians: Exploring Paul's Letters
ISBN 1-55945-146-7

Applying the Bible to Life, ISBN 1-55945-116-5

Becoming Responsible, ISBN 1-55945-109-2

Bible Heroes: Joseph, Esther, Mary & Peter
ISBN 1-55945-137-8

Boosting Self-Esteem, ISBN 1-55945-100-9

Building Better Friendships, ISBN 1-55945-138-6

Can Christians Have Fun?, ISBN 1-55945-134-3

Caring for God's Creation, ISBN 1-55945-121-1

Christmas: A Fresh Look, ISBN 1-55945-124-6

Competition, ISBN 1-55945-133-5

Dealing With Death, ISBN 1-55945-112-2

Dealing With Disappointment, ISBN 1-55945-139-4

Doing Your Best, ISBN 1-55945-142-4

Drugs & Drinking, ISBN 1-55945-118-1

Evil and the Occult, ISBN 1-55945-102-5

Genesis: The Beginnings, ISBN 1-55945-111-4

Guys & Girls: Understanding Each Other
ISBN 1-55945-110-6

Handling Conflict, ISBN 1-55945-125-4

Heaven & Hell, ISBN 1-55945-131-9

Is God Unfair?, ISBN 1-55945-108-4

Love or Infatuation?, ISBN 1-55945-128-9

Making Parents Proud, ISBN 1-55945-107-6

Making the Most of School, ISBN 1-55945-113-0

Materialism, ISBN 1-55945-130-0

The Miracle of Easter, ISBN 1-55945-143-2

Miracles!, ISBN 1-55945-117-3

Peace & War, ISBN 1-55945-123-8

Peer Pressure, ISBN 1-55945-103-3

Prayer, ISBN 1-55945-104-1

Reaching Out to a Hurting World, ISBN 1-55945-140-8

Sermon on the Mount, ISBN 1-55945-129-7

Suicide: The Silent Epidemic, ISBN 1-55945-145-9

Telling Your Friends About Christ, ISBN 1-55945-114-9

The Ten Commandments, ISBN 1-55945-127-0

Today's Faith Heroes, ISBN 1-55945-141-6

Today's Media: Choosing Wisely, ISBN 1-55945-144-0

Today's Music: Good or Bad?, ISBN 1-55945-101-7

What Is God's Purpose for Me?, ISBN 1-55945-132-7

What's a Christian?, ISBN 1-55945-105-X

FOR SENIOR HIGH:

1 & 2 Corinthians: Christian Discipleship
ISBN 1-55945-230-7

Angels, Demons, Miracles & Prayer, ISBN 1-55945-235-8

Changing the World, ISBN 1-55945-236-6

Christians in a Non-Christian World
ISBN 1-55945-224-2

Christlike Leadership, ISBN 1-55945-231-5

Communicating With Friends, ISBN 1-55945-228-5

Counterfeit Religions, ISBN 1-55945-207-2

Dating Decisions, ISBN 1-55945-215-3

Dealing With Life's Pressures, ISBN 1-55945-232-3

Deciphering Jesus' Parables, ISBN 1-55945-237-4

Exodus: Following God, ISBN 1-55945-226-9

Exploring Ethical Issues, ISBN 1-55945-225-0

Faith for Tough Times, ISBN 1-55945-216-1

Forgiveness, ISBN 1-55945-223-4

Getting Along With Parents, ISBN 1-55945-202-1

Getting Along With Your Family, ISBN 1-55945-233-1

The Gospel of John: Jesus' Teachings
ISBN 1-55945-208-0

Hazardous to Your Health: AIDS, Steroids & Eating Disorders, ISBN 1-55945-200-5

Is Marriage in Your Future?, ISBN 1-55945-203-X

Jesus' Death & Resurrection, ISBN 1-55945-211-0

The Joy of Serving, ISBN 1-55945-210-2

Knowing God's Will, ISBN 1-55945-205-6

Life After High School, ISBN 1-55945-220-X

Making Good Decisions, ISBN 1-55945-209-9

Money: A Christian Perspective, ISBN 1-55945-212-9

Movies, Music, TV & Me, ISBN 1-55945-213-7

Overcoming Insecurities, ISBN 1-55945-221-8

Psalms, ISBN 1-55945-234-X

Real People, Real Faith, ISBN 1-55945-238-2

Responding to Injustice, ISBN 1-55945-214-5

Revelation, ISBN 1-55945-229-3

School Struggles, ISBN 1-55945-201-3

Sex: A Christian Perspective, ISBN 1-55945-206-4

Today's Lessons From Yesterday's Prophets
ISBN 1-55945-227-7

Turning Depression Upside Down, ISBN 1-55945-135-1

What Is the Church?, ISBN 1-55945-222-6

Who Is God?, ISBN 1-55945-218-8

Who Is Jesus?, ISBN 1-55945-219-6

Who Is the Holy Spirit?, ISBN 1-55945-217-X

Your Life as a Disciple, ISBN 1-55945-204-8

Order today from your local Christian bookstore, or write: Group Publishing, Box 485, Loveland, CO 80539.